GW00367879

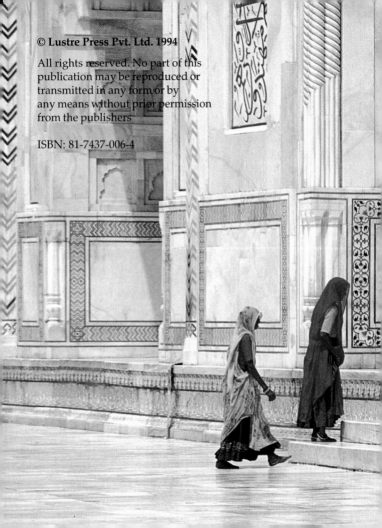

ISBN: 81-7437-006-4

# Taj Mahal

Promodini Varma

## Lustre Press

Delhi ◇ Banaras ◇ Agra ◇ Jaipur ◇ The Netherlands

# Taj Mahal

*I*n their 180 years of effective rule, the Mughals wrote one of the most glorious chapters in Indian history, and even though Shah Jahan, the fifth in line, may not have been the greatest of the Mughals, he was certainly the grandest. The third son of Jahangir, Shah Jahan, the 'Ruler of the World' ascended the throne in 1627 at the age of 36, after a bloody war of succession. Within four years, however, his favourite wife and inseparable companion for 19 years, the beauteous Mumtaz Mahal, the 'Chosen One of the Palace', had died, giving birth to their fourteenth child. The death of Mumtaz, who had been loving, generous, kind and supportive, left the emperor deeply depressed. He mourned her for two years, denying himself all ostentation and luxury. He built the Taj Mahal as a mark not only of the beauty and character of his wife but also as a monument to their love.

Work commenced on the Taj in 1632, within a year of the death of Mumtaz. Many models must have been submitted to the emperor but historians are now agreed that no single person can be credited with having created

*Out of the morning mist, across the shimmering waters, there rises the pearly dome and minarets of the Taj Mahal like 'a house not made with hands'.*
**Facing page:** *A winter morning view from a spot east of the Taj.*

the blue-print for the most exquisite mausoleum on earth. The chief inspiration and the final word must have been that of Shah Jahan, who even as a young boy of 15 had given proof of his architectural abilities by redesigning the living quarters assigned to him at Kabul. In his later buildings at Delhi and Agra, he would further refine that fruitful commingling of the Hindu and Islamic styles into what would come to be known as the Mughal style. In the Taj he would achieve perfection.

Like many other Mughal mausoleums, the Taj, is a garden tomb. The distinguishing feature of a Mughal garden is the

*Preceding pages:*
*The Taj, which took twenty-two years*
*(1632-54) to build is a magnificent example of meticulous*
*planning and execution. The main vista is along a sandstone*
*water course set between rows of trees leading to a marble*
*platform. (A view from the top of the main gate now closed to*
*visitors.)* **This page:** *Inlay work on top of Shah Jahan's*
*cenotaph.* **Facing page:** *Details from the base of the dome. Inlay*
*work was done by artists from South India.*

10

water that gurgles and cascades over scalloped marble terraces. In the Taj, in keeping with the serene mood of the monument, the play of water is kept to a minimum, being confined to the fountains that dissect the raised rectangular marble pond and the water channels. The channels are broad, glistening sheets of water, calm and quiet, and the central pool reflects back the sombre Taj.

The garden, an expanse of green in the typical *charbagh* style (rectangle divided into 4 equal parts) interposes itself between the outer gate and the main monument, so that the pearly white of the Taj is framed between the green of the grass and the blue of the sky. The tomb itself is square in design, with chamferred corners so that no sense of angularity remains. Set on a marble plinth, each of the four facades has a huge central arch flanked by a set of smaller arches, one on top of the other, on either side. On the chamferred corners are another set of arches, built on a semi-octagonal base so that they are visible from both the adjacent fronts. Each section of the facade is marked by slender pilasters of varying heights that end in lotus

bud finials. The entire facade is decorated with beautiful inlaid work and inscriptions from the Koran. At the four corners of the plinth, detached from the central structure, rise four round minarets on octagonal bases each crowned with a single *chhatri*.

Inside, the double-storeyed structure of the exterior is maintained in the Taj. The large central hall, which contains the sepulchres of Mumtaz Mahal and Shah Jahan, is octagonal in shape and has 4 rectangular rooms alternating with 4 octagonal rooms at the sides, all connected with a corridor. All the sides, except the south entrance, are closed with delicately perforated marble screens filled with translucent glass so that only a very dim light can filter into the interior. To this diffused natural light is added the soft glow of candles that burn on the cenotaphs and the rays that stream down from the Egyptian lamp that hangs from the ceiling, presented in 1909 by Lord Curzon, the one Viceroy who did much to preserve India's cultural heritage from both Indian and European plunderers.

The tombs, made of translucent white marble inlaid with precious stones, sometimes as many as 48 pieces to a flower to achieve the right shades, are decorated with

*Facing page:* On the head of the illuminated sepulchre of Mumtaz Mahal is inscribed a passage from the Koran 'GOD is HE beside whom there is no god. He knoweth what is concealed and what is manifest. He is merciful and compassionate.'

arabesque and floral patterns. That of Mumtaz Mahal, with Koranic inscriptions and a slate lies in the centre of the hall. That of Shah Jahan, lying off-centre bears the inscription: 'The sacred sepulchre of the Most Exalted Majesty, Dweller of Paradise, the Second Lord of Constellation, the King Shah Jahan, may his mausoleum ever flourish, 1706 Hijri.' The cenotaphs in the crypt below are replicated in the main hall. It is the crypt which houses the real graves, the final resting places of Mumtaz Mahal and Shah Jahan. In the upper hall, the cenotaphs are surrounded by a delicately carved and inlaid octagonal marble screen.

The chief beauty of the mausoleum is, of course, the dome which, in spite of being huge and majestic, gives the impression of floating on air. It is a double dome, the outer shell designed to harmonize with the outer dimensions of the building and the inner shell designed to fit in with the hall inside. On the outside the dome rests on a drum, which gives it the appearance of a neck. At the base of the dome are four *chhatris* to balance the extraordinary height of the dome.

On either side of the main mausoleum are two identical red sandstone structures each topped by three marble domes. The structure on the west is a mosque; the structure on the east a Mehman Khana or a Caravan Sarai. The two buildings are locally also called *sawal–jawab* or query and response. The design of the buildings echoes the Taj in muted fashion, replicating the arches, domes and ornamentation of the main mausoleum.

It is said that Shah Jahan planned another mausoleum for himself on the opposite bank of the river Yamuna. However, it is certain that not even Shah Jahan could have built another Taj, for 'The Taj truly is . . . a poem. It is not only a pure architectural type, but also a creation which satisfies the imagination, because its characteristic is Beauty.'

*A fine example of inlaid work on the octagonal screen surrounding the cenotaphs. Made of a single piece of marble, inlaid with precious stones such as jaspers, agates and bloodstones set in a hundred ways, forming the most 'beautiful and precious style of ornament ever adopted in architecture'.*

15

Passing over a pavement you enter a great gateway of red freestone elaborately carved and inscribed with sentences from the Koran. Slowly, as the semi-vault whose arch hangs high above is passed, a descent by a flight of steps reveals before your eyes the lovely Taj—an eternal communion of love and devotion.
**Facing page:** Full view of the Taj Mahal from the Gateway.
**Above:** Main Gateway to the Taj made of red sandstone with inlay work.

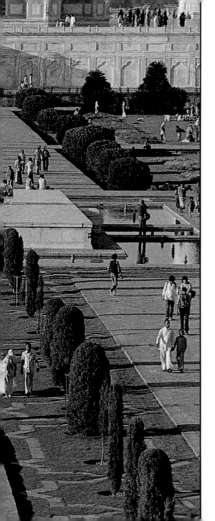

Six months after Mumtaz's death, on a Friday morning, her body was taken to Agra. The site selected for the mausoleum was the garden of Raja Jai Singh of Jaipur. She remained buried in a temporary resting place for 22 years before her body was removed to the present tomb on which is built the Taj Mahal.

Between the gateway and the Taj itself is a spacious marble platform in the centre of which sparkles a lovely fountain and a row of jets deau placed some feet from each other, carried from end to end with a beautiful walkway on both sides.

View of the charbagh style garden with marble platform in the centre. Notice the row of fountains from one end to the other.

***Facing page and Above:*** *The construction started in 1632, one year after the death of the empress. There are conflicting reports as to who was the chief architect, Ustad Ahmed Lahori or Isa Muhammad Afandi from Turkey. A verse composed by Shah Jahan himself and inscribed on the Taj reads: 'The builder could not have been of this earth. For it is evident the design was given him by heaven.'*

*Millions of visitors from all walks of life come to see this wonder of the world.*

Ismail Afandi from Turkey built the dome, Mohammad Hanif from Baghdad was the master-mason, Qazim Khan from Lahore cast the finial and Amanat Khan from Shiraz was the calligrapher. Chiranji Lal was the chief of mosaic work. They were paid a salary ranging from Rs 600 to Rs 1000 (£ 12 to £ 18) per month. The names of some of the artisans appear at the entrance to the tomb and the gateway.

The Taj was constructed under the supervision of Makramat Khan and Mir Abdul Karim. White marble came from Jaipur and yellow from the banks of the river Narbada, crystal from China and lapis lazuli from Sri Lanka. Other stones such as cornelian came from Baghdad, turquoise from Tibet, agate from Yemen, coral from the Red Sea, onyx from Persia, and chrysolite from Europe. Yet the official cost of construction was put at a mere Rs 50 lacs (£ 100 000).

**Preceding pages:** *Full view of the Taj.*

**Facing page and This page:** *Sadhus and Maulvis, both find peace in the serenity of the mausoleum.*

The corners of the main building are chamferred to relieve angularity and relate the minarets to the whole structure in a way that would not have been as elegant had the structure remained a perfect square.

A view of the chamferred corners and the minarets.

As one examines each part, one is astonished at the grandeur of the soul that planned and the genius that executed so marvellous a task. At each angle of the terrace stands a minaret, 133 feet in height, of most exquisite proportions, built of white marble, surmounted by a light, graceful cupola supported on eight elegant pillars and reached by a spiral staircase now closed to visitors.

A view of the top of the minaret.

On the entrance, from the pavement to the
top, are inserted passages from the Koran in
letters of black marble inlaid with such
exactness that if you pass a needle point
over the stone, it will not be interrupted.
Each letter, so inserted, is about a foot in
length. 'Cut out with a precision and
elegance that the best calligraphist could
not produce, with pen on paper'.
**Facing page and Above:** The entrance to
the main hall where both Shah Jahan and
Mumtaz are buried.

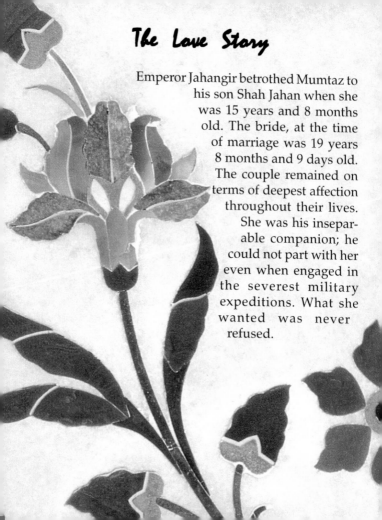

# The Love Story

Emperor Jahangir betrothed Mumtaz to his son Shah Jahan when she was 15 years and 8 months old. The bride, at the time of marriage was 19 years 8 months and 9 days old. The couple remained on terms of deepest affection throughout their lives. She was his inseparable companion; he could not part with her even when engaged in the severest military expeditions. What she wanted was never refused.

Shah Jahan had fourteen children by Mumtaz of whom eight were sons and six daughters. It was in giving birth to her fourteenth child, a girl, that the empress died.

Mulla Lahori, the author of the *Badshah Nama* and Mohammad Saleh of *Amal-i-saleh* written in the seventeenth century have given a touching account of the last moments of the empress.

*Mumtaz Mahal*
*1593-1631*

On 8 June 1631, late at night, Shah Jahan was summoned by his favourite daughter Jahanara. The queen, after delivering a healthy baby girl had taken a turn for the worse. The emperor hastened to the queen's tent and sat at the head of his dying wife. Mumtaz

*The real tomb in a low vault beneath the upper hall.*

looked on the emperor with despair and tears in her eyes and admonished him to take good

34

*Shah Jahan*
*1592-1665*

sunrise Mumtaz died while Shah Jahan gazed into her eyes. The emperor slumped by the bed and wept inconsolably.

Shah Jahan's life changed for ever. For nineteen years, Mumtaz Mahal had been his most trusted advisor and companion, never

care of her children and her own aged parents when she was no more. She also whispered to him to build a monument symbolizing the sublime beauty of their eternal love. Three hours before

once leaving his side.

The entire Kingdom mourned. For two years Shah Jahan's empire went without music, public entertainment, perfumes or brightly coloured clothes. The magnificent ruler had lost sparkle. It was gloom all over.

Shah Jahan shut himself from the world, refused food and drink and abandoned all pleasurable pursuits for two years. Those who were near him could hear the great emperor moan continuously through the night. Shah Jahan's hair turned completely white during this emotional ordeal.

*The emperor and Mumtaz Mahal are burried beside each other. A view of the cenotaphs in the upper hall.*

Over the cenotaph of Mumtaz Mahal is a slate; over that of Shah Jahan an ink well, for it was believed that a man would inscribe the desires of his soul on the heart of the woman and she would fulfil them in heaven as she had done on earth.

Verses from the Koran inscribed on Mumtaz Mahal's cenotaph.

Ink well over Shah Jahan's cenotaph.

Shah Jahan's cenotaph.

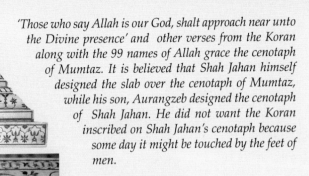

'Those who say Allah is our God, shalt approach near unto the Divine presence' and other verses from the Koran along with the 99 names of Allah grace the cenotaph of Mumtaz. It is believed that Shah Jahan himself designed the slab over the cenotaph of Mumtaz, while his son, Aurangzeb designed the cenotaph of Shah Jahan. He did not want the Koran inscribed on Shah Jahan's cenotaph because some day it might be touched by the feet of men.

*Mumtaz Mahal's cenotaph.*

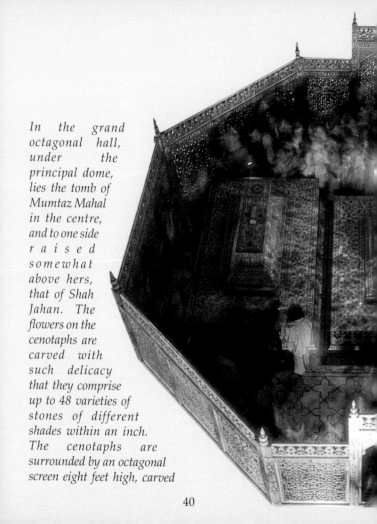

In the grand octagonal hall, under the principal dome, lies the tomb of Mumtaz Mahal in the centre, and to one side raised somewhat above hers, that of Shah Jahan. The flowers on the cenotaphs are carved with such delicacy that they comprise up to 48 varieties of stones of different shades within an inch. The cenotaphs are surrounded by an octagonal screen eight feet high, carved

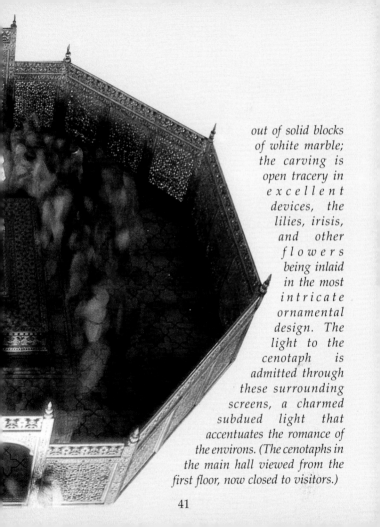

out of solid blocks of white marble; the carving is open tracery in *excellent devices*, the lilies, irisis, and other *flowers* being inlaid in the most *intricate ornamental design*. The light to the cenotaph is admitted through these surrounding screens, a charmed subdued light that accentuates the romance of the environs. (The cenotaphs in the main hall viewed from the first floor, now closed to visitors.)

41

*After Mumtaz, much of Shah Jahan's life was spent in the middle of a bloody war of succession waged by his four sons. His third son Aurangzeb, having killed or captured his brothers, declared himself emperor. Shah Jahan was imprisoned in Agra Fort, barely a kilometre away from the Taj Mahal across the river Yamuna. Shah Jahan survived eight mournful years in a marble apartment in this fort from where he would sit staring at the monument he had built for his beloved.*

***Preceding pages and This page:*** *View of the Taj Mahal from Agra Fort next to the apartment where Shah Jahan was imprisoned.*

*Shah Jahan died in the winter of 1665. His body was brought down from the fort through the watergate to the river Yamuna. The cortege sailed solemnly to the Taj Mahal where he was buried next to his beloved wife. On the opposite bank of the river from the Taj are the ruins of an old foundation where Shah Jahan had intended to build a mausoleum for himself replicating the Taj. But Aurangzeb ordered that his father be buried next to his mother, thwarting Shah Jahan's plans.*

*Picture shows the fort from where Shah Jahan's body was ferried to the Taj Mahal through the waters of the Yamuna.*

***Facing page and Above:*** *Flanking the Taj Mahal is a mosque and a* Mehman Khana *(guest house) often termed as* sawal–jawab *(query and response). Besides their distinct purposes, the two structures were built to provide symmetry to the main monument. Though built of red sandstone, the inlaid mosaic work on them (as exhibited above) is of a very high order.*

*The sight of the Taj by moonlight is most entrancing. The whole structure appears to sparkle like a diamond. The pure white dome, raised on a marble platform, viewed from a distance, looks like a brilliant pearl. The calm stream flowing by its side, coupled with the soft shadow cast by the trees, adds to the loveliness of the scene. Nothing but a whispering breeze breaks the surrounding calm.*

***Facing page, Above and Following pages:*** *On a full moon night Taj Mahal viewed at 8 pm, 10 pm and midnight.*

'Did you ever build a castle in the air? Here is one brought down to earth, and fixed for the wonder of ages; yet so light it seems, so airy, and, when seen from a distance, so like a fabric of mist and sun beams, with its great dome soaring up, a silvery bubble, about to burst in the sun.'

*The Taj viewed on a misty morning in winter.*

'How excellent the sepulchre of the lady of Bilquis's fame,
That a cradle for the body of the princess of the world became.
Like a garden of heaven a brilliant spot,
Full of fragrance like paradise fraught with ambergris....
The sight of this mansion creates sorrowing signs,
And makes the sun and moon shed tears from their eyes.'

Shah Jahan's own composition in praise of the Taj Mahal in the Badshah Nama a seventeenth century manuscript by Abdul Hamid Lahori.